D1224236

Author:

Peter Cook has worked as a designer and art director in publishing for 30 years. He has written *You Wouldn't Want to Sail on a 19th Century Whaling Ship!* and created the electronic version of the **You Wouldn't Want to Be** series.

Artist:

David Antram was born in Brighton, England, in 1958. He studied at Eastbourne College of Art and then worked in advertising for fifteen years before becoming a full-time artist. He has illustrated many children's non-fiction books.

Series Creator:

David Salariya was born in Dundee, Scotland. He has illustrated a wide range of books and has created and designed many new series for publishers both in the UK and overseas. In 1989, he established The Salariya Book Company. He lives in Brighton with his wife, illustrator Shirley Willis, and their son Jonathan.

Editor:

Sophie Izod

© The Salariya Book Company Ltd MMVI

Published in Great Britain in 2006 by
Book House, an imprint of
The Salariya Book Company Ltd
25 Marlborough Place, Brighton BN1 1UB

ISBN 0-531-12422-3 (Lib. Bdg.)
ISBN 0-531-12447-9 (Pbk.)

Published in 2006 in the United States
by Franklin Watts
An imprint of Scholastic Library Publishing
90 Sherman Turnpike, Danbury, CT 06816

A CIP catalog record for this book is available from the Library of Congress.

Printed and bound in China.

You Wouldn't Want to Be at the Boston Tea Party!

Wharf Water Tea You'd Rather Not Drink

Written by
Peter Cook

Illustrated by
David Antram

Created and designed by
David Salariya

Franklin Watts®
A Division of Scholastic Inc.
NEW YORK • TORONTO • LONDON • AUCKLAND • SYDNEY
MEXICO CITY • NEW DELHI • HONG KONG
DANBURY, CONNECTICUT

Contents

Introduction

The year is 1773. Your name is George Robert Twelves Hewes and you were born in Boston, Massachusetts, in 1742. You have grown up in a time of turmoil, when American colonists are first beginning to rebel against the unjust rule of the British government. You are at the center of some of the most important events in U.S. history. These events will lead to the American Revolution, an eight-year-long struggle against the might of the British Empire. Eventually you and your fellow Americans will win your freedom, and a new nation will be born: the United States of America.

But all this lies in the future. On the night of December 16, 1773, you are busy blacking your face with coal dust and disguising yourself as a Mohawk Indian. You are about to take part in the strangest "tea party" of all time. It is a night that will change American history forever.

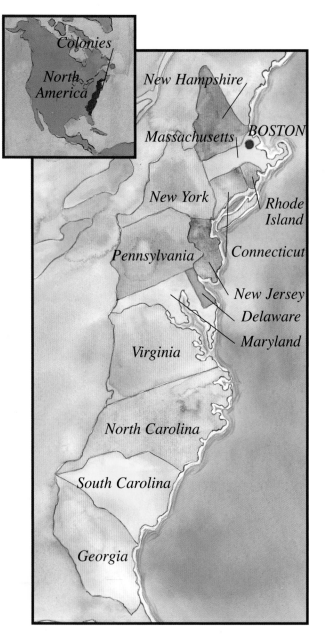

THE THIRTEEN COLONIES. Boston is the capital of Massachusetts, one of 13 colonies established by British settlers on the east coast of North America during the 17th century. The colonies have their own form of local government but are subject to laws and taxes imposed by the British Parliament.

Boston: Cradle of Independence

In 1773 Boston is one of the most important cities in North America. It has a population of 15,000, and it is a major port for all trade to and from the Old World. Boston is about to become the center of the struggle against British rule. Several of its citizens will become key figures in the coming revolution, including Samuel Adams, John Hancock, and Paul Revere. Like most other Bostonians, you don't care much about politics. You simply want to make a living as a shoemaker. But you resent the British soldiers (known as redcoats) who are stationed in your town. The presence of the soldiers and the burden of British taxes angers you and many of your fellow citizens.

Your Early Life:

One of 9 children, you became an orphan at 14 and have always been poor. You apprenticed as a shoemaker but earn little money. When you try to join the British army you are rejected because you are just 5 feet, 1 inch tall. Things are so bad that you've even spent time in a debtor's prison.

A POOR ORPHAN

ARGUING
WITH A REDCOAT.
You make a pair of shoes
for a British soldier, but he
refuses to pay for them.
Many Bostonians are
mistreated in similar
ways by the British.

Handy Hint

Don't argue with British soldiers stationed in the town. You could be beaten up, or even worse!

APPRENTICE SHOEMAKER

TOO SHORT FOR THE ARMY

IN DEBTOR'S PRISON

No Taxation Without Representation!

In 1763 Britain and France sign a treaty to end the French and Indian War. This gives the British control of Canada and makes the American colonies secure from attack by the French and their Indian allies. But the war has cost a great deal of money, and the British Parliament votes to tax the colonists to help pay for the cost of defending them. Over the next few years Parliament passes the Sugar Act in 1764, the Stamp Act in 1765, and the Townshend Acts in 1767 to raise money by taxing various goods. This leads to protests and the soon-to-be familiar cry of "No taxation without representation!" American colonists are not represented in the British Parliament, and they have no say in any of the laws it passes.

Taxing the Colonists:

THE SUGAR ACT (left). Many goods imported into the colonies became subject to tax, including sugar, coffee, wine, glass, paint, paper and tea.

THE STAMP ACT (right). Direct taxes were imposed on legal documents, newspapers and other printed materials. "Stamp Masters" were appointed to collect taxes.

HANG HIM!
An effigy of a
Stamp Master hangs
from Boston's famous
"Liberty Tree."

Handy Hint

If you want to keep your friends, don't become a Stamp Master!

BURN HIM! A mob burns down the house of Governor Hutchinson, who supports the taxes.

The Boston Massacre

Boston becomes the center of discontent with British rule, so the British government stations 4,000 troops in the city—about one soldier for every four civilians. On the afternoon of March 5, 1770, a group of boys begins throwing snowballs at a sentry guarding the customs house. You are among the crowd that gathers to watch the fun. When the sentry summons help, a squad of 8 soldiers confronts the crowd and opens fire, killing five civilians. You are standing next to James Caldwell, one of the victims, and catch the dying man in your arms. The soldiers are eventually put on trial, but only two are found guilty. Their hands are branded to show they are guilty of manslaughter—a light punishment that enrages all Bostonians.

What Led to the Massacre:

TEN DAYS before the massacre a crowd surrounded the house of Ebenezer Richardson, who was an informer to British troops. Richardson fired into the crowd, killing an 11-year-old boy. His funeral was attended by over 2,000 Bostonians.

TWO DAYS before the massacre some off-duty British soldiers are beaten up by Bostonians (above). This angers the British, many of whom want revenge.

Handy Hint

Don't make British soldiers angry—they may shoot you!

BOYS throw snowballs at a sentry who calls for help (above).

A CROWD GATHERS. As more snowballs are thrown, the soldiers fire at the unarmed civilians (above right). Three are killed on the spot, and two die later from their wounds.

CRISPUS ATTUCKS is one of those killed. He is believed to have been an African-American. Some historians view him as the first casualty of the American Revolution.

11

Sons of Liberty

When the American colonists first protest against the new taxes, few consider independence from Britain. They simply want to be treated fairly and to have some control over the laws and taxes imposed on them by a distant government. But the Boston Massacre fuels a growing resentment against British rule. Citizens begin to band together to oppose new taxes. One group in New York call themselves the Sons of Liberty, and soon other colonies follow their lead and form their own Sons of Liberty groups. You attend meetings held under the famous "Liberty Tree," but at that point you have no idea where the cries of "Liberty!" will lead.

Means of Communication:

HANDBILLS (left). Printed handbills are an important part of the anti-British propaganda campaign run by the Sons of Liberty.

COURIERS (right). Committees of Correspondence are set up to send messages between the American colonies. These messages are carried by couriers on horseback.

"Liberty!"

Handy Hint
Don't get caught giving out handbills or you might be sent to prison!

SAMUEL ADAMS (right) is a Boston lawyer, and leader of the Sons of Liberty in Massachusetts. Adams is a firm believer in colonists' rights.

TARRED AND FEATHERED (left). The Sons organize boycotts of merchants who import British goods. They also harass customs officials, some of whom are tarred and feathered by angry colonists.

The Tea Tax

After the Boston Massacre the British try to appease the colonists: troops are withdrawn from Boston and all major import taxes are removed, except for the tax on tea. The colonists begin to buy British goods again, but not tea! The 1773 Tea Act removes the tax, but sales are controlled by "tea agents." This leads to cheaper tea, but the colonists still oppose the new law. You aren't a tea drinker, but you join the crowds at the Liberty Tree on November 3 to demand that the tea agents resign. Fearing for their lives, the agents ask Governor Hutchinson to take over. By the end of the month the British tea ship *Dartmouth* sails into Boston Harbor.

The British East India Company:

TEA PLANTATIONS (right). Tea imported into America comes from plantations in India owned by the British East India Company. The British government wants its company to have control of all tea sold in America.

TEA AGENTS (right). American merchants are worried that if the British can appoint tea agents, they can do the same for other goods. This would mean that they could control trade and even ruin American businesses.

TEA DRINKING.
Although all classes drink tea, it is a ritual in middle- and upper-class homes where ladies serve tea in fine cups made of china or porcelain.

Handy Hint

Get used to drinking coffee. Tea is going to be in short supply!

A Growing Rebellion

With the arrival of the first tea ship, over 5,000 people gather at the Old South Meeting House to hear the leaders of the Sons speak. It is agreed that the tea must not be landed, and the ships should return to Britain. You are in the crowd and watch as two more tea ships dock in the harbor. The tea remains on board, but Governor Hutchinson has set a date of December 17 for the cargo to be unloaded under the protection of British soldiers. On the 16th, a huge crowd gathers, determined to stop the tea from landing on American soil.

How Events Unfold:

THE *DARTMOUTH* (above) arrives in Boston Harbor on November 27, but the crowd prevents its cargo of tea from being unloaded. She is joined by two other British tea ships, the *Eleanor* and the *Beaver*.

GOVERNOR HUTCHINSON (above) is determined that the tea will land. He knows if a ship isn't unloaded within 20 days of entering port, its cargo can be seized. The governor plans to use this law, enforced by British soldiers.

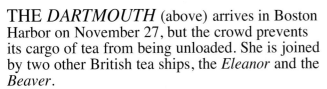

Handy Hint

Wear a disguise to avoid being spotted at the tea party!

OLD SOUTH MEETING HOUSE
(left). Built in 1729 as a Puritan meeting house, it is the largest meeting space in colonial Boston. Important meetings of the Sons of Liberty take place here on November 30 and December 16, 1773. When he hears about Governor Hutchinson's refusal to let the tea ships return to Britain, Samuel Adams tells the crowd, "This meeting can do nothing more to save the country."

INSIDE THE MEETING.
Some are dressed as Indians, ready for the action about to take place that night. Roth arrives to tell them of the Governor's decision. The tea party is about to begin . . .

FRANCIS ROTH,
son of the *Dartmouth's* owner, rides to Hutchinson's house outside Boston to seek permission for the ship's return to Britain with its cargo of tea. The governor refuses.

17

The Boston Tea Party

The Sons decide that the tea must be destroyed. Around 30 men are set this task. They dress as Mohawk Indians to avoid being recognized. About 100 more, including you, join them. Your job is to board a ship and demand the keys for its hold. The captains hand over the keys, and the "Indians" lift the tea chests onto the deck. They split open 342 tea chests on 3 boats with hatchets and tip the contents into the sea. It takes three hours to complete. A huge crowd cheers you on from the dockside.

Boston Harbor is a teapot!

18

TEA PARTY SONG.
"Rally Mohawks!
Bring your axes,
and tell King George
we'll pay no
taxes on his
foreign tea!"

Handy Hint

Don't steal any
British tea.
The crowd
might
lynch you!

Tea Thief!

You spot Captain O'Connor trying
to steal tea, which the Sons have
forbidden. His coat tears as you
grab him, but he escapes and is
chased by the crowd.

Captain O'Connor

THE PIECE of torn coat is nailed to a
whipping post to shame O'Connor.

Punishment from London: The Intolerable Acts

When news of the tea party reaches Britain, the King and Parliament are outraged. A series of laws, known as the Intolerable Acts, are passed to punish the colonists. Boston Harbor is closed, the powers of the Massachusetts government are reduced, and the colonists are ordered to provide housing for British troops. The people of Boston are angered by this latest outrage from London and know they must make a stand to defend their liberty. But many loyalists still support the British, and you are about to encounter one of them!

A Loyalist Encounter:

YOU STOP John Malcolm, a known loyalist and customs informer, from beating a boy. He strikes your head with his cane, knocking you unconscious.

LED BY THE Sons of Liberty, a crowd drags Malcolm from his house and takes him to the Liberty Tree, where he is tarred and feathered.

REVENGE! Angry members of Parliament pass the Boston Port Act, closing the harbor until the tea is paid for.

Handy Hint

Don't get into a fight with loyalists. You could get hurt!

"Mad" King George

KING GEORGE III (1738–1820) is the British monarch during and after the events leading up to the American Revolution. He supports the strong measures against the colonists, stating that "We must master them or leave them to themselves." In later life he suffers from periods of poor health and insanity believed to be caused by an illness called porphyria.

The British Are Coming!

t is hoped that the Intolerable Acts will end rebellion in the colonies, but they have the opposite effect. In September 1774, the First Continental Congress is attended by representatives from 12 of the 13 colonies. They protest about the new laws and urge the colonists to arm themselves to defend their rights. General Gage, now governor of Massachusetts, enforces the new laws and is determined to capture your leaders. Hundreds of British troops search the town for weapons and smuggled goods. Paul Revere warns Samuel Adams and John Hancock of the British plan to arrest them. They escape, but local militia decide to oppose the British troops and fight for liberty.

PAUL REVERE (right).
A Boston silversmith and engraver, Revere is a leader of the Sons who took part in the Boston Tea Party. He is also a courier for the Massachusetts Committee of Correspondence.

REVERE'S RIDE (right).
On the night of April 18/19, 1775, Revere rides 16 miles from Charlestown to Lexington to warn other leaders of the Sons of Liberty that the British are marching to arrest them.

LEXINGTON

CONCORD

British route

Revere's route

BATTLES OF LEXINGTON AND CONCORD. On April 19, 75 colonial militia confront 700 British troops on Lexington Green. Shooting begins; eight militia are killed and ten wounded. The British then march to Concord to destroy arms supplies. But word spreads, and thousands of colonists begin to converge on the town. Now outnumbered, the British make a fighting retreat back to Boston.

Boston Besieged:
The Battle of Bunker Hill

The British retreat from Concord inspires other patriots to converge on Boston from towns throughout Massachusetts and the surrounding colonies. By June 1775, American general Artemas Ward leads 15,000 volunteers, who lay siege to 6,400 British troops in Boston. On June 16 the Americans take up a position on the heights of Charlestown peninsula, controlling access to Boston Harbor. General Gage sends in 2,400 British troops to force them out, and by the next day a pitched battle takes place. The Americans are driven from the peninsula, but the British lose over 1,000 men compared to 450 American casualties. The British troops in Boston are evacuated in 1776.

THE MINUTEMEN (left) are a local militia organized to oppose the British. They are known as Minutemen because they could be called to arms at a minute's notice. You want to join them, but the British stop all able-bodied men from leaving Boston to join the patriots.

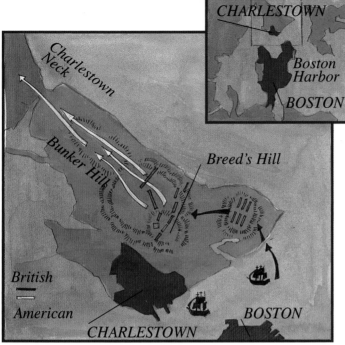

Boston
Harbor

BOSTON

Charlestown
Neck

Bunker Hill

Breed's Hill

British

American

CHARLESTOWN

BOSTON

THE BATTLE OF BUNKER HILL (above). British forces land and advance on Breed's Hill. Two attacks are repulsed, but a third drives the Americans back along the peninsula. You watch the battle from across the bay.

THE REDCOATS (right) are so called because of the color of their uniform. Many of the "British" troops are actually German! King George III has German ancestry, and up to 30,000 Hessians (from the German region of Hesse) are fighting for the British.

Handy Hint

Throw away any red clothes, in case you're mistaken for a redcoat!

The American Revolution

The Battle of Bunker Hill is the first major engagement in what will become an eight-year-long struggle for American independence. General George Washington is appointed commander of the Continental Army, which fights the British in the northern colonies. The British dominate the opening years of the war by capturing New York and Philadelphia. But the Americans are now determined to win their liberty, and on July 4, 1776, the Declaration of Independence is approved by the Continental Congress. The United States of America is born, but the war continues. You escape from Boston in 1775 and meet George Washington, who is planning to recapture the city. You volunteer to fight and spend many months at sea as well as serving as a private in the militia.

BATTLES AT SEA. Sailing from Boston, you fight aboard a privateer—a privately owned ship employed to fight the British. Boston is the center of the American navy and during the war captured ships are sailed into the town's harbor.

LIBERTY BELL. The symbol of American independence, the Liberty Bell (above), rings out after the Declaration of Independence is signed in Philadelphia.

CROSSING THE DELAWARE. On Christmas night 1776, Washington and 2,500 soldiers cross the icy Delaware River. They surprise the British and win battles at Trenton and Princeton. These important early victories boost American morale.

STARS AND STRIPES The 13 stars and stripes on this American flag represent the original 13 colonies.

DECLARATION OF INDEPENDENCE. Drafted by Thomas Jefferson, this document outlines the principles of independence, and includes the rights to "Life, Liberty, and the pursuit of Happiness."

A New Nation

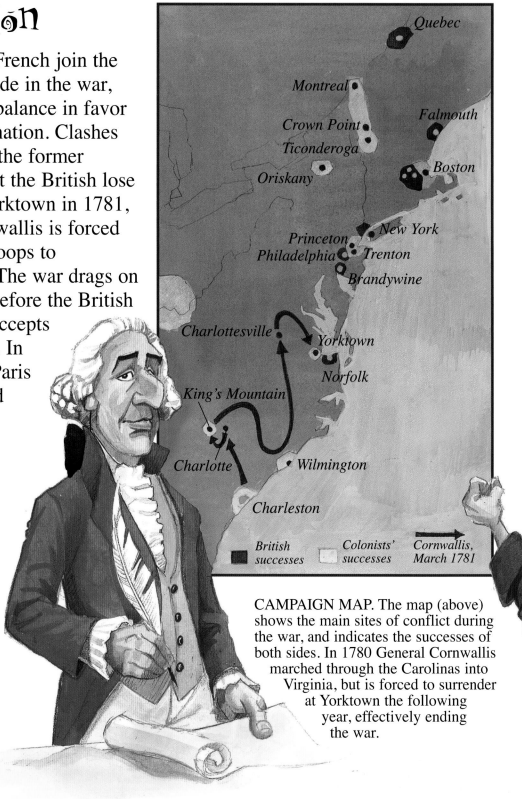

In 1778 the French join the American side in the war, tipping the balance in favor of the new nation. Clashes continue in the former colonies, but the British lose a critical battle at Yorktown in 1781, where General Cornwallis is forced to surrender 8,000 troops to Washington's army. The war drags on for two more years before the British government finally accepts that they cannot win. In 1783, the Treaty of Paris ends the conflict, and Britain formally recognizes the independence of the United States of America.

Quebec

Montreal

Crown Point

Ticonderoga

Falmouth

Oriskany

Boston

Princeton

New York

Philadelphia

Trenton

Brandywine

Charlottesville

Yorktown

Norfolk

King's Mountain

Charlotte

Wilmington

Charleston

British successes

Colonists' successes

Cornwallis, March 1781

GEORGE WASHINGTON (right). As commander in chief of the Continental Army, Washington defeats the superior British forces. A grateful Congress elects him as the first president of the United States in 1789.

CAMPAIGN MAP. The map (above) shows the main sites of conflict during the war, and indicates the successes of both sides. In 1780 General Cornwallis marched through the Carolinas into Virginia, but is forced to surrender at Yorktown the following year, effectively ending the war.

WHEN THE WAR ENDS you do not return to Boston, as the British have burned down your shop. You and your wife move to a nearby town, where you will have 16 children. But the part you played on the night of December 16, 1773, will not be forgotten. You live to the great age of 98 and become famous as one of the last living survivors of the Boston Tea Party.

Handy Hint

Don't forget to celebrate Independence Day each year on July 4th!

A CENTENARIAN (below). Your portrait now hangs in the library of the Bostonian Society. It is wrongly called *A Centenarian* because it was believed at the time that you were over 100 years old.

INDEPENDENCE DAY (above). You become a popular figure at Independence Day celebrations held on the Fourth of July.

Glossary

Brand A mark burned on the skin of a criminal as a punishment.

British East India Company A trading company that was chartered by the British government in 1600 to develop trade in Asia.

Centenarian A person who lives for 100 years.

Continental Congress The first government of the United States of America, formed in 1774.

Courier A person carrying messages.

Customs A duty or tax imposed on imported goods.

Debtor Someone who owes money to another person or company.

Handbill A printed document or pamphlet delivered by hand.

Liberty Tree An ancient elm on the corner of Essex Street and Orange Street in Boston. It was a focal point for anti-British meetings.

Lobster back A colonist's nickname for British soldiers, whose red coats were like the color of a boiled lobster.

Loyalists American colonists who did not want independence from Britain.

Militia A military force composed of civilians who can be called upon for emergency service.

Mohawk A tribe of Indians native to what is now New York State.

Porphyria An inherited disease that can cause mental confusion.

Privateer A privately owned ship and its crew, who are authorized by a government to attack and capture enemy ships during wartime.

Sons of Liberty (also referred to as The Sons within the text). An organization founded in November 1765 to oppose the Stamp Act.

Tar-and-feather A punishment in which a person's body is smeared with tar and then coated with feathers (which stick to the tar).

Whipping Post A post set up in a public place. Criminals are tied to it to be whipped.

Index